APHRODISIAS

BKG

APHRODISIAS
Bilkent Kültür Girişimi Publications

PREPARATION FOR PUBLICATION

Author
Orhan Atvur

Project Coordinator
Hakime Özgüven

Translation and Editing
Michael D. Sheridan

Art Consultant
Gürol Sözen

Graphic Design Director
Erkal Yavi

Management Unit Director
Alev Taşkın

Photographs
Cem Aydın
Mutlu Yılmaz

Design Application
Deniz Ünal
Gürhan Zan

Map
Metin Keskin

Coordination and Production
Korpus Kültür Sanat Yayıncılık Tic. Ltd. Şti.
Hüsrev Gerede Cad. Soydan Apt. 80/4 Teşvikiye-İstanbul/Turkey
Tel: +90 212 236 71 61 - 62
info@korpus.com.tr

Printing
Promat Baskı Yayın San. ve Tic. A.Ş.
Sanayi Mah. 1673 Sok. No: 32 Esenyurt, Büyükçekmece-İstanbul/Turkey
Tel: +90 212 622 63 63 - +90 212 605 07 98
www.promat.com.tr

ISBN 978-605-5495-11-4
Printed Date: June 2011

CONTENTS

5 INTRODUCTION

6 HISTORY

7 THE CITY PLAN

8 MONUMENTS OF THE ANCIENT CITY OF APHRODISIAS

10 THE THEATER

16 THE TETRASTOON AND THE THEATER BATHS

24 THE SOUTH AGORA (PORTICO OF TIBERIUS) AND THE AGORA GATE

30 THE CIVIL BASILICA

35 HADRIAN'S BATHS

40 THE NORTH AGORA

42 THE BOULEUTERION (COUNCIL HOUSE) AND THE ODEON

47 THE BISHOP'S PALACE

49 THE SCULPTORS' ACADEMY

50 THE TEMPLE OF APHRODITE AND THE BASILICA CHURCH

56 THE STADIUM

63 THE MONUMENTAL GATE (TETRAPYLON)

68 THE SEBASTEION

74 THE APHRODISIAS MUSEUM

View of Afrodisias from the air.

INTRODUCTION

Aphrodisias lies on a plateau 600 meters (1,968 feet) above sea level, 13 kilometers (8 miles) east of Karacasu in Aydın Province. It is 100 kilometers (62 miles) distant from the city of Aydın and 80 kilometers (50 miles) distant from the city of Denizli. To the east of Aphrodisias lies the 2,375-meter (7,792-foot) Babadağ Mountain, which was known as Salbakos in antiquity and whose snows have been a blessing to the people of the Geyre Plateau for centuries.

The Dandalaz River flows to the south of the plateau before turning west to empty into the legendary Menderes River 25 kilometers (16 miles) below. Meandering through this valley of civilizations, the Menderes River finally exhausts itself in Karine, near the ancient city of Miletus, bringing the greetings of the goddess Aphrodite down to the Aegean Sea, from which this great city of Caria was born.

Aphrodisias is the city of Aphrodite, the goddess of love. However, the goddess of Aphrodisias is not the Aphrodite with whom we are most familiar. Rather, this Aphrodite is in fact the Mother Goddess of fertility, emerging from the depths of history and first known to us from the Neolithic period. She is Cybele, the Earth Mother of the Phrygians on Anatolian soil, her cult statue—found in the Temple of Aphrodite as well as being on display in the Aphrodisias Museum—akin to the Artemis of Ephesus.

In the year 1959, the arrival of a young Turkish archaeologist in Aphrodisias changed not only this young man's fate, but the fate of the city as well. This young man was Professor Kenan T. Erim, whose name has today become virtually synonymous with Aphrodisias. Prof. Erim explains his first arrival in Aphrodisias like this:

"When I took to the road from Nazilli in July of 1959, I couldn't have imagined how important a journey this was going to be. Before getting as far as Geyre on a very rough dirt road out of Karacasu, I saw the pillars of the Temple of Aphrodite. The village had completely swallowed up Aphrodisias, but it was nonetheless unable to conceal its wonders. Before evening, I returned to Nazilli. In my room in the only hotel in the district, I remember writing this: 'This will be a whole new era in my life.'"

It was this day that was the beginning of Prof. Erim's passion for Aphrodisias, which grew greater and greater all throughout the years, until he passed away on 3 November 1990. In line with a wish expressed in his last will and testament, and by special permission of the Turkish government, stating that those who had performed outstanding service to cities of antiquity could be interred within the city they had thus served, Prof. Erim was buried beside the tetrapylon of the monumental gate of Aphrodisias.

Since 1991, archaeological digs and research at Aphrodisias have been continued under the auspices of New York University.

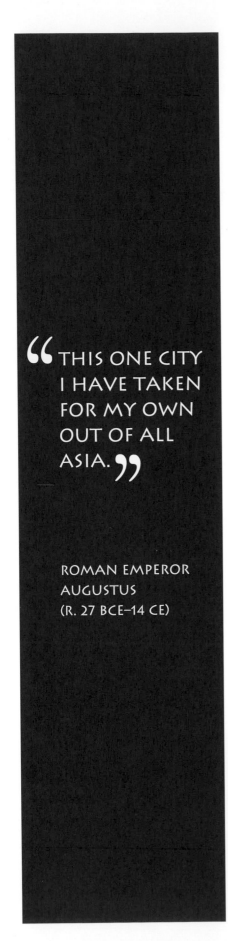

HISTORY

The first settlement at Aphrodisias dates back to approximately seven thousand years ago, during the Neolithic period. Settlement continued in the area through the Chalcolithic period and the Bronze and Iron Ages. Covered up by the later settlement of the city of Aphrodisias, these prehistoric settlements were found on the hill of the Acropolis, along whose slope the theater lies, and on Pekmez Hill to its east.

According to the Byzantine historian Stephanus, Aphrodisias' original name was Lelegonpolis. It later took the name Megapolis, and still later Ninoi, after the Assyrian ruler Ninus. It is to this latter period that we can ascribe the arrival in Aphrodisias of Aphrodite, goddess of love: the Assyrians, their cities destroyed by the Medes and Babylonians, came from Nineveh to this distant region, bringing with them the cult of Ishtar, the Mesopotamian goddess of love. This event, long considered no more than legend, has recently been confirmed through the discovery of a relief on the Aphrodisias excavation site. On this relief, found in the Civil Basilica, we can see figures representing Ninus and his legendary wife Semiramis.

The first historical documents relating to Aphrodisias date to the 3rd century BCE, and are found in the history of Caria written by Apollonius of Aphrodisias. In the 2nd century BCE, the city maintained its alliance with the neighboring city of Plarasa (today's Bingeç Köyü) by minting common money. Although the remains of different, prior settlements have been discovered, it is only in the 1st century BCE that Aphrodisias first emerges as a city. In the year 82 BCE, the Roman general Sulla

sent to the Temple of Aphrodite as a gift a golden crown and a double-bladed ax, the latter being considered holy in Caria. This shows that the city had grown in importance in parallel with Roman hegemony in Anatolia. In an inscription dating to this period, there is mention of two Aphrodisians who traveled to Rome as plaintiffs for the cities of Asia (*i.e.*, Anatolia) in order to complain of the oppression inflicted by officials collecting taxes in the name of Rome; the Aphrodisians, according to the inscription, were treated with great honor in all the cities through which they traveled. In 39–35 BCE, Marcus Antonius granted approval for tax exemption status for Aphrodisias and Plarasa. In approximately 30 BCE, with the establishment of the Roman Empire under Augustus, Aphrodisias became a prosperous and famed city.

In the Byzantine era, Christianity did not immediately come to hold sway over the city, with polytheism continuing in a number of places. When Christianity did become dominant in Aphrodisias, however, the city's statues were broken and discarded, and in the 6th century CE, the city took the name Stauroupolis, meaning "City of the Cross". It was in this period that the Temple of Aphrodite was converted to a church.

In the 11th century, the upper steps of the ancient theater were ripped out and the Acropolis was used as a castle. In the 13th century, this castle was besieged by the Seljuks, and, after having changed hands several times, finally came under firm Seljuk control. Around the end of the 18th century, the area was settled by nomadic Turks, taking the name Geyre, a corruption of "Caria". Following an earthquake in 1956, this village founded upon the ruins of Aphrodisias was relocated two kilometers (1.2 miles) to the east, thanks to the efforts of Professor Kenan T. Erim.

Currently, Aphrodisias, which is among the best preserved and protected of Turkey's historical sites, receives an average of 150,000 visitors annually.

THE CITY PLAN

Aphrodisias is located in the region known in ancient times as Caria. It lies at a distance of 180 kilometers (112 miles) from the city of Ephesus (modern Efes) and 100 kilometers (62 miles) from Hierapolis (modern Pamukkale). Founded atop the Geyre Plateau 600 meters (1,968 feet) above sea level, Aphrodisias was, at the time of its initial founding, a small village comprising solely a temple and the small houses constructed around it. In the 1st century CE, it began to undergo urbanization upon the return to the city of Zoilos, a manumitted slave of Augustus, and work was begun on the current temple as well as on the theater. It is these two edifices that formed the foundation of ancient Aphrodisias as it stands today, and the city was subsequently developed between these two monuments.

The two hills within the city—the Acropolis on whose slope the theater rests and, to the east of this, Pekmez Hill—are the two tells or conical mounds containing the city's previous settlements, dating back to seven thousand years ago. The eastern part of the Acropolis tell was destroyed while the theater was being constructed. The walls surrounding the city were built rather hastily during the Gothic raids of the year 360 CE.

Prior to this date, the Temple of Aphrodite was considered to be protecting the city, and so no need was felt for protective walls. When such walls did come to be seen as necessary, time was short, and so the walls were built largely using stone gleaned from other structures and monuments that had become dilapidated over time; this is why we can still see a number of inscriptions on the wall and its various structures.

The walls contain six gates in the eastern, western, and northern sections, three of which are especially large gates. The main roads leading in from these gates are not all visible today. In the Byzantine era, new structures were built atop some of the roads, and the city plan underwent great changes. For instance, in the 7th century CE, a three-apsed church was built at the junction where the road running westwards from the eastern gate turns north. Additionally, in this period certain roads had houses built upon them, thus closing these roads to passage. Recent geophysical and geomagnetic studies in Aphrodisias have confirmed these findings, and it has been determined that the 3.5-kilometer-long (2-mile-long) walls enclose an area of approximately 520 hectares (1,285 acres). These hastily built walls underwent repairs in the 5th century CE.

Beginning in the 17th century, Western travelers and researchers began to revisit Aphrodisias. In 1812, the Society of Dilettanti—made up of British architects and illustrators—did some work in the city of Aphrodisias and drew up the first design plan of the city. In 1835, the famed traveler Charles Texier performed research at Aphrodisias, eventually publishing his findings in his work *Description de l'Asie Mineure*.

In 1892, Osman Hamdi Bey—director of Istanbul's Royal Museum (*Müze-i Hümâyûn*)—traveled to Aphrodisias and decided to undertake an archaeological dig here, though this plan never came to fruition.

The first dig at Aphrodisias was undertaken in 1904–05 by the French railroad engineer, amateur archaeologist, and collector Paul Gaudin. Gaudin, however, was obliged to leave the site early, and the second year of this work was completed by Gustave Mendel. Another dig was begun in 1913 by André Boulanger, but was brought to a halt by the outbreak of World War I. The Italian Giulio Jacopi undertook to continue the work on Aphrodisias in 1937, but this time the excavation was left only half completed as a result of the outbreak of World War II.

Most of the work at Aphrodisias has been done on the Temple of Aphrodite, Hadrian's Baths, and the Portico of Tiberius. Organized, continuous work at Aphrodisias was begun in 1961 by Professor Kenan T. Erim under the auspices of New York University, and this work was continued without significant stoppage until Prof. Erim's death on 3 November 1990.

During this period, the village of Geyre, sitting right atop the ancient city, was relocated to the plateau to the west, allowing the remains that can now be seen to finally come into the light of day. As one result of this work, countless articles and studies on Aphrodisias saw publication. Today, excavation at Aphrodisias continues under the auspices of New York University.

MONUMENTS OF THE ANCIENT CITY OF APHRODISIAS

1 THE THEATER
2 THE TETRASTOON AND THE THEATER BATHS
3 THE SOUTH AGORA (PORTICO OF TIBERIUS) AND THE AGORA GATE
4 THE CIVIL BASILICA
5 HADRIAN'S BATHS
6 THE NORTH AGORA
7 THE BOULEUTERION (COUNCIL HOUSE) AND THE ODEON
8 THE BISHOP'S PALACE
9 THE SCULPTORS' ACADEMY
10 THE TEMPLE OF APHRODITE AND THE BASILICA CHURCH
11 THE STADIUM
12 THE MONUMENTAL GATE (TETRAPYLON)
13 THE SEBASTEION
14 THE APHRODISIAS MUSEUM

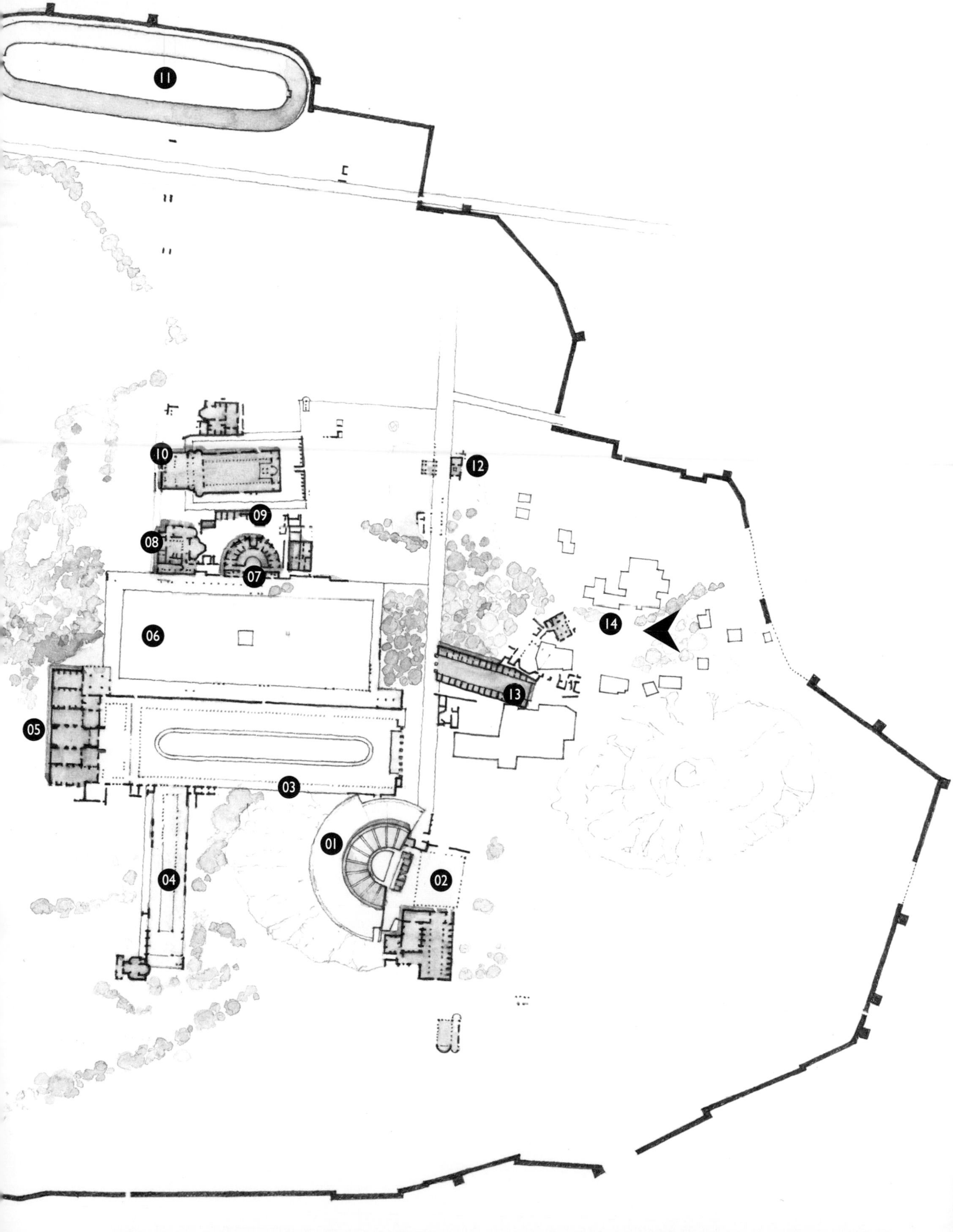
01
02
03
04
05
06
07
08
09
10
11
12
13
14

1. THE THEATER

The development of the city of Aphrodisias was begun with the construction of the Temple of Aphrodite, the North Agora, and the Theater.

In 1961, the 30-year-old researcher Professor Kenan T. Erim, one of the most important names in studies of the ancient city of Aphrodisias, initiated the Aphrodisias Archaeological Research and Excavation project under the auspices of New York University. At the time, the village of Geyre—now located two kilometers (1.2 miles) to the west of Aphrodisias—lay directly atop the ancient city. Before excavation on the theater was begun, the 55 homes and a mosque lying atop the ancient structure were nationalized and moved to their new location. Excavation on the theater began in the year 1966. So much earth had collected over the structure that, when excavations uncovered fully upright and stable seating, the archaeologists were truly surprised to have found such a sturdy and well-preserved theater.

Roman theaters were typically built so as to descend down along a natural slope. Such was also the case with the theater of Aphrodisias, which was constructed by digging into the eastern part of the ancient tell or conical mound of the Acropolis, thus creating a slope there.

Three main sections comprise the theater: the stage building (*skene*), the orchestra, and the seating area (*cavae*).

The Aphrodisias Theater, constructed entirely of marble, is one of Anatolia's ancient structures.

The stage building: The stage building, or *skene*, is a three-storey structure. From the first storey upwards to the third storey, the three storeys were built according to, respectively, the Doric, Ionic, and Corinthian styles. As we learn from an inscription on the superstructure of the first storey, the stage building was "constructed on the order of Zoilos, manumitted slave of the son of Caesar (Octavianus), and dedicated to Aphrodite, to Rome, and to the City."

On the building's second and third storeys, numerous statues were used as decorative elements between the columns and in the niches. A figure of Apollo, two figures of the muse of tragedy Melpomene, two figures of boxers, statues representing Demos and Nike, and a bust of the Aphrodite of Aphrodisias were unearthed during the excavation of the theater, and are currently on display in the Aphrodisias Museum. The private rooms of the actors and the backstage area, where various accessories and equipment were stored, are also on the first floor, and can still be seen today.

In front of the stage building lies the large stage, or *proskenion,* where the actors would perform plays.

The orchestra: The semi-circular area in front of the stage building was known as the orchestra. In older theaters, when there was as of yet no stage building, plays would be staged in this area. In Roman theaters, orchestras were constructed, although plays would still be performed on the forestage. During the time of the Roman emperor Marcus Aurelius (r. 161–180 CE), a portion of the lower seating was removed and the orchestra was dug out as a pit. In this area, also called the

konistra, gladiatorial and wild beast competitions would be held. For a time during the later Roman period, circus games would also take place in this area.

The seating area (*cavae*): There are two seating areas, or *cavae*, in the theater, one lower and one upper, among which were walkways known as *diazoma.* Only the lower seating area has survived to the present day. Following an earthquake in the 7th century, the theatrical function of the upper seating area and the stage came to an end. The steps of the upper seating area were

The theater, the lower seating area, and the stage building, with the Tetrastoon in the background.

Bust of Aphrodite
In this 2nd-century CE work discovered in the theater and now on display in the museum's Hall of Aphrodite, the goddess Aphrodite, protectress of the city, is depicted with a headpiece in the form of city ramparts. The laurel wreath round her forehead symbolizes abundance and peace. In statuary of the Roman period, the goddess Aphrodite was portrayed as a religious symbol. This bust gives us an idea of what the head of the now headless cult statue of Aphrodite that stands opposite it may have looked like.

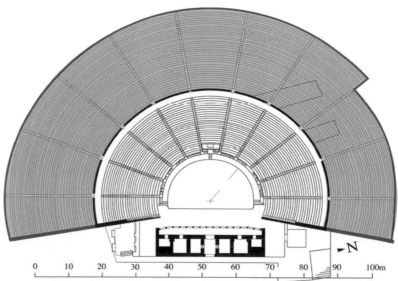

N

| 0 | 10 | 20 | 30 | 40 | 50 | 60 | 70 | 80 | 90 | 100m |

First storey of the theater's stage building, in the Doric style.

Inscription on the architrave of the first storey of the stage building, discussing Zoilos' dedication of the building to Aphrodite, Rome, and the people.

the city, and private letters—make it one of the most important documents of Anatolian archaeology. As an example, one of the inscriptions mentions a golden statue of Eros that was presented to the temple as a gift by Caesar, and was later stolen and taken to the Temple of Artemis in Ephesus before being recovered. The names Aphrodisias and Aphrodite were removed from the inscriptions following the city's acceptance of the Christian religion.

The most important and well known of the inscriptions on the Archive Wall is a letter laudatory of Zoilos and written by Octavianus—later known as Emperor Augustus—to the governor Stephanus of Laodicea during the authority vacuum following the assassination of Julius Caesar:

"CAESAR TO STEPHANUS, GREETINGS. YOU KNOW MY AFFECTION FOR MY FRIEND ZOILOS.

I HAVE FREED HIS NATIVE CITY AND RECOMMENDED IT TO ANTONIUS. SINCE ANTONIUS IS ABSENT, TAKE CARE THAT NO BURDEN FALLS UPON THEM.

THIS ONE CITY I HAVE TAKEN FOR MY OWN OUT OF ALL ASIA.

I WISH THESE PEOPLE TO BE PROTECTED AS MY OWN TOWNSMEN.

I SHALL BE WATCHING TO SEE THAT YOU CARRY OUT MY RECOMMENDATION TO THE FULL."

used in the construction of the castle atop the hill, while the lower seating area was used as a garbage dump.

The entire structure is built of marble. Among the more interesting remains are the graffiti carved in the lower seating area. At stage level of the lower seating area lies a private lodge, built at a later date.

There are also numerous inscriptions carved in the Greek alphabet onto the north wall of the stage building; this wall is popularly known as the "Archive Wall". Its contents—including letters written by the Roman Senate, concessions granted to

2. THE TETRASTOON AND THE THEATER BATHS

Over the centuries, Aphrodisias has experienced numerous earthquakes. The traces of these earthquakes can be seen in the repairs carried out on the city's ancient structures. In cases where repair proved impossible, new structures would be built. Following an especially violent earthquake in the 4th century CE that resulted in flooding of the low-lying parts of the city, a new agora or marketplace was constructed to the east of the theater. This area was named the Tetrastoon, meaning "four arcades", by archaeologists. As this marketplace was small, certain sellers—having purchased places there for themselves—inscribed their names in the flooring, in which a sun dial is also located. In the middle of the agora is a fountained pool. Some of the architectural decorations unearthed during the excavation of the theater's stage building can also be found here.

The floored and vaulted passage connecting the Tetrastoon to the east-west street has been named the "Hall of Emperors" owing to the numerous statues of emperors unearthed during excavations here. Also among the interesting remains are the the pilasters, carved with the characteristic reliefs of Aphrodisias' sculptors' workshop. Along both sides of the passage lie small shops.

The Tetrastoon, the Hall of Emperors, and the Theater Baths.

Blue-gray marble columns in the Hall of Emperors.

Statue of a priestess of Aphrodite with a bust of Aphrodite on the band on her head.

The Tetrastoon and the Theater.

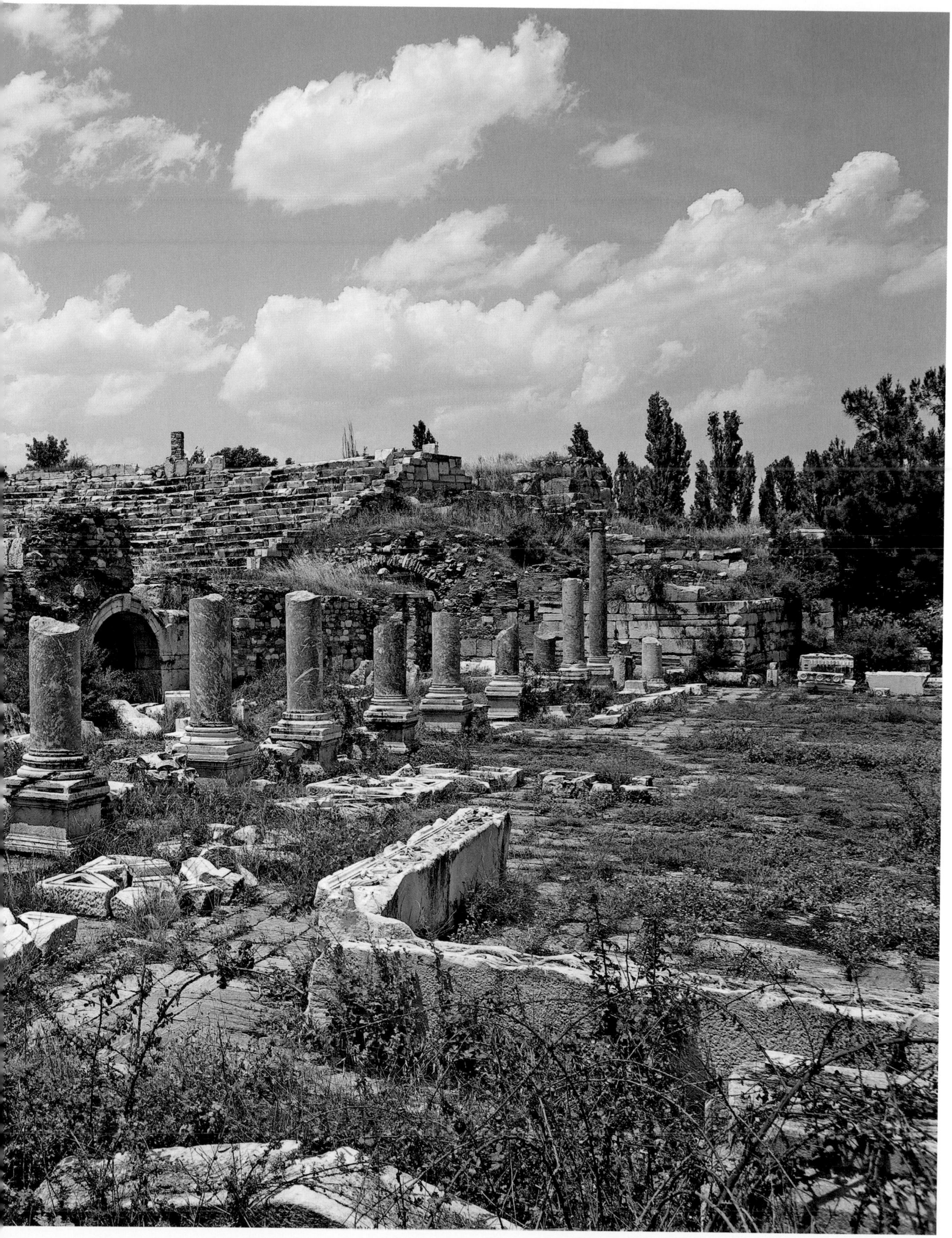

The Theater Baths' calidarium (hot baths).

The baths located between the Hall of Emperors and the theater have been named the "Theater Baths" as a result of their being adjacent to the latter. This structure—excavation on which has not yet been completed—is different from Aphrodisias' other monumental structures in that it was not built of large blocks. Mortar was used in the cementing together of its small, smooth stones. The baths' hot bath section, or *calidarium,* is covered by a dome, which is quite out of the ordinary for such a structure. Apart from the *calidarium,* we can also see the sweating room (*sudatorium*) and the changing room (*apodyterium*). Work has not yet begun on the baths' other sections. Those sections that have come to light have flooring laid with marbles of various colors.

The Theater Baths' apodyterium *(changing room).*

The Theater Baths.

The South Agora, the North Agora, and the Temple of Aphrodite, with the stadium and city walls in the background.

Emperor Tiberius, depicted as a god, with a slave (Sebasteion relief).

3. THE SOUTH AGORA (PORTICO OF TIBERIUS) AND THE AGORA GATE

In cities under Roman rule, whenever a new emperor came to power, new structures dedicated to the new emperor would be built in the city. On occasion, emperors would grant financial assistance for the building of such structures. Construction on the South Agora, located in the space between the southern end of the North Agora and the northern edge of the theater, was begun in the time of Emperor Tiberius (r. 14–37 CE), and so this, together with the inscription on the architrave on the South Agora's northern side, has led us to call this structure

The acropolis and the western side of the Portico of Tiberius.

The Agora Gate with the small pool, later used as a fountain, in its front.

*Friezes on the Portico of Tiberius
(South Agora), depicting various
gods, goddesses, and portrait heads.*

*The rich artwork and elevated subjects
of the Portico of Tiberius friezes.*

the "Portico of Tiberius". We can understand from the portico's remains that it was an unfinished structure. Its construction was also interrupted from time to time by earthquakes. The friezes on the upper part of the structure, with their excellent worksmanship and great variety, are important in terms of both quantity and quality. The garland-decorated friezes are on display before the front wall of the excavation team's headquarters.

The structure on the east of the portico is called the Agora Gate. It was originally constructed as a monumental gate, but its entrances were later sealed off and a pool placed in its front so that it could be used as a fountain. The vaulted passageways on both sides of this fountain connected the portico to the north-south road.

In the center of the portico is a large pool 260 meters (853 feet) in length, 25 meters (82 feet) in width, and 1.20 meters (3.94 feet) in depth. Judging from the very numerous bits of piping in the vaulted passage on the north side of this pool, it seems probable that it was built as a necessity to collect the waters that emerged following an earthquake in the 2nd century. Underneath the theater-like seats ranged around the pool is a canal that could empty the pool's excess water into the sewer system. Though there are some who claim that the pool's water was used for the baths to its west, this seems unlikely due to the difference in elevation between the two structures.

The exact function of this whole structure—whether it saw use as a gymnasium or simply as a promenade—is still debated by archaeologists.

The Portico of Tiberius and the eastern edge of the pool in its center.

4. THE CIVIL BASILICA

The rectangular building stretching southwards from the southwestern corner of the South Agora is the Civil Basilica. Basilicas are rectangular structures whose interior is divided into two rows of columns and a nave. Though Roman basilicas were originally public, non-religious buildings used as courtrooms and by administrators, soldiers, and state officials, they served in Christian times as examples for churches built on the basilical plan.

The Civil Basilica of Aphrodisias began with a monumental entrance opening onto the South Agora. On the front face of the entry building, price lists would be scratched into the marble in such a way that they could be seen from the agora. Dated to the year 301 CE and known as Emperor Diocletian's Edict on Maximum Prices, these lists were made so as to put a cap on prices, which were rising rapidly as a result of inflation brought on by the minting of unbacked money. Besides the food, drink, and various other products sold in the agora, prices for services were also laid out in detail here. To give some examples: 1 bushel of wheat was 100 *denarii,* 1 bushel of rice was 200 *denarii,* the daily fee for a carpenter was 50 *denarii,* and 1 shave was 2 *denarii.* Because coins continued to be minted, however, these lists—as well as the imperial edict itself— were not actually in effect for very long.

The entrance to the Civil Basilica from the Portico of Tiberius and the columns of the basilica's naves.

Beyond the entrance, in the central nave, a statue of blue-gray marble known as the "Blue Horse" was discovered. The statue, together with its still intact base, was moved to the museum after its discovery, and is now on display in the Sevgi Gönül Hall. The statue depicts a horse running at a full gallop; of the horse's rider, only the left calf remains. In the south wall of Aphrodisias we find the following inscription:

"THE PEOPLE ERECTED TROILOS, THE HORSE, AND ACHILLES."

The base of the statue supports the possibility that the Blue Horse was just one part of a three-part group of statues depicting an incident from the Trojan War: the young Trojan prince Troilos leaves the safety of the walls of Troy on his horse, and Achilles drags him down off of the horse by his hair as the boy rides by at a full gallop. The rider of the horse was made of white marble, and was mounted on a bronze saddle with gold leaf meant to represent a tiger pelt. However, only the iron pins holding the saddle have survived to the present day, and no part of the Achilles figure has been discovered.

The panels on the balustrades above the rows of columns on the north of the central nave are decorated in relief. With depictions of and inscriptions concerning Ninus and Semiramis, these panels are quite interesting and important works in terms of the mythical origins of the city of Aphrodisias.

In recent years, excavations have unearthed a high-quality portrait head from the large room on the south side of the basilica, which connects to the east-west road.

The Civil Basilica.

The Blue Horse statue, discovered behind the entrance of the Civil Basilica.

5. HADRIAN'S BATHS

The Roman emperor Hadrian (r. 117–138 CE) visited Aphrodisias on one of his journeys to Anatolia, and the city's council had these baths constructed as a memorial of his visit. The baths are made up of two large sections where the men and the women would bathe separately. Directly in front of the entrance on the north side is a marble pool ornamented with statues and with large pillars at the corners. The parallel rooms directly to the right are, in order, the changing room (*apodyterium*), the cold baths (*frigidarium*), the warm baths (*tepidarium*), and the hot baths (*calidarium*). The complicated galleries and corridors beneath the structure formed the building's heating system, known as the *hypocaust*. The structure is built primarily of sandstone covered with marble paneling. The front courtyard of the building, the *palaestra,* is particularly highly ornamented on the beams and entablature lying between its pilasters.

The marble elements of the building are decorated in acanthus leaves—a specialty of Aphrodisias' sculpting academy—among which we can see figures of Eros, people, and animals. The enormous heads of mythological figures that formed the edges of the entablature are currently on display before the walls of the garden at the museum's entrance.

The open-air pool between the palaestra *and the main structure.*

The open-air pool, with columns at its four corners and surrounding statues.

Hadrian's Baths.

The first excavation on Hadrian's Baths was undertaken in the year 1904 by the French railroad engineer Paul Gaudin. A portion of the works unearthed in the course of this excavation were moved to the Istanbul Archaeology Museum, while some were removed from the country without permission. Professor Kenan T. Erim proved, for example, that the torso part of the fisherman's head that he discovered at the Portico of Tiberius in 1989 had been sold to Berlin's Pergamon Museum by Gaudin's heirs, and he began official processes to attempt to have this work returned to Aphrodisias.

The pilaster friezes of the palaestra, *which are distinctive works of the Aphrodisias school of sculpting.*

6. THE NORTH AGORA

In the ancient Greek world, the marketplace where city shops could be found and where daily foodstuffs could be purchased was called the agora. In the agoras, all varieties of shopping and trade were carried out. Both the trade and the prices in the agoras were controlled by the agora's administrator.

In Aphrodisias in the 1st century BCE, the area between the Temple of Aphrodite and the theater, then under construction, was planned out carefully. It was on the southern end of this space that the Portico of Tiberius would later be constructed, while the southwestern end would be taken up by Hadrian's Baths.

The North Agora of Aphrodisias occupies the space between the Bouleuterion, or Council House, and the Portico of Tiberius. This distinctive structure is surrounded by columns on all sides. Some of the columns, supporting Ionic-style capitals, have remained standing in the western and eastern corners. Standing beside tall poplar trees as though vying with them to climb up to the heavens, these columns can be easily seen from the top of the theater. On the northern side of the agora, a small entry building connects the marketplace to the Bouleuterion. The pool directly in the center of the agora once

The North Agora, with Hadrian's Baths in the background.

had a fountain, and numerous coins were uncovered here during excavation; thus, it may have been used as a place of devotional offerings. The base of the large pool in the southwestern corner was laid with marble, and there were steps descending into the pool at the corners. On the eastern side are doorframes and lintels that have remained standing.

Columns of the southwestern portico of the North Agora.

7. THE BOULEUTERION (COUNCIL HOUSE) AND THE ODEON

Located between the Temple of Aphrodite and the agora, the Bouleuterion or Council House was constructed in the 2nd century CE. The upper part of the current seating area was destroyed in an earthquake in the 4th century CE. This same earthquake was the cause of flooding in the city: because of the flooding, the Bouleuterion's bottom two rows of seats were removed; the floodwaters gathered here and the pool that was thus formed prevented damage to the building's foundations. The water gathered here was emptied out into the sewer system beside the agora by means of pipes. The odeon, with a capacity to seat 1,750 people in its upper area, was covered by a roof of wood and tile. A number of statues representing philosophers stood in the niches of the two-storey stage building, and the porticoed hall leading from behind the stage out to the North Agora was also decorated with statues.

In ancient Greek cities, the bouleuterion was the meeting hall of the city council. It would also, however, be used for concerts; dance, pantomime, and rhetorical performances; and poetry readings.

To the west of the Bouleuterion is the memorial gravesite of a well-known Aphrodisian, a building with an older circular plan surrounded by columns and with a sarcophagus in its center. A portion of the first steps of the grave's podium section lies underneath the Bouleuterion building.

The Bouleuterion, the lower seating area, and the orchestra (pool), with the Temple of Aphrodite in the background.

*The orchestra, the stage building, and
the lower seats of the Bouleuterion.*

The Bouleuterion's stage building and the gangway
(parodos) *leading to the Bishop's Palace.*

The Bouleuterion's stage building.

The Bouleuterion's agora entrance.

Back hallway of the Bouleuterion.

Circular memorial gravesite, constructed earlier than the Bouleuterion.

8. THE BISHOP'S PALACE

When moving northwards from Hadrian's Baths but before reaching the Bouleuterion, we see on the left a quite well-preserved building built to a three-apse plan; this is known as the Bishop's Palace. Built using rubble and small stone blocks, this structure was originally built in the 5th and 6th centuries CE to serve as a guesthouse for governors of the united provinces of Caria and Phrygia, but when the provincial system was later done away with it came to be used by the bishops of the area. The building consists of several different rooms, with the blue-gray columns in its courtyard having been brought from Aphrodisias' marble quarries. At the beginning of the year 2000, comprehensive conservation work

The courtyard of the Bishop's Palace, with the columns of the Temple of Aphrodite on the left.

was carried out on the structure, and around the same time a doctoral dissertation concerning the structure was written.

Statue of the young Hercules.

9. THE SCULPTORS' ACADEMY

In the Hellenistic period, Pergamon served as one of the more important sculpting academies in Anatolia. Kings and rulers were the patrons and protectors of all artists. Among the most generous of kings was Attalos III (r. 138–133 BCE), the last king of Pergamon, who left his entire kingdom to Rome in his will upon his death. When the kingdom thus passed to Rome, this patronage vanished, and the kingdom's sculptors scattered to the four corners of Anatolia, with an important portion of them relocating to Aphrodisias. Today, scholars universally accept that the Aphrodisias Sculptors' Academy was active from the 1st century BCE to the beginning of the 6th century CE. The end of these sculpting workshops came when Christianity became dominant and the city's name was changed to Stauroupolis.

Many of the statues that have been unearthed in excavations bear the signatures of Aphrodisian sculptors. In fact, certain masters— such as Koblanos, Apollonius, Antoninos, Aristeas, Papias, Zenin, and Zenon the son of Alexander—eventually went to the imperial capital of Rome to create statues there. As is known, sculptors in the Roman period generally followed the style of Classical and Hellenistic artists. Aphrodisian sculptors, however, produced many high-quality and unique works of their own. A large role in the production of the Aphrodisias school's numerous excellent statues was played by the high-quality marble quarries located approximately one kilometer (0.6 miles) to the north of the city. Archaeologists estimate that at least 2,000 statues were produced in the city.

Based on unfinished statues and study pieces unearthed in the excavations, we can say that the Aphrodisias Sculptors' Academy was located between the Bouleuterion and the Temple of Aphrodite, and an inscription discovered in recent years seems to prove this. Owing to the fact that, in later eras, the Sculptors' Academy saw use as an olive oil factory, and later as a private residence, traces of the excellent work produced there have largely been destroyed. It is therefore much easier to comprehend the number and quality of the school's works by visiting the Aphrodisias Museum.

The Sculptors' Academy later saw use as an olive oil factory.

10. THE TEMPLE OF APHRODITE AND THE BASILICA CHURCH

The remains of the temples built for the different gods and goddesses in whom a city believed in antiquity have, despite the ravages of centuries, at least partially survived to our own day. In Aphrodisias, there are two temples that we know of: the Temple of Aphrodite, which gave a name to the city, and the Sebasteion complex, dedicated to the Roman emperors.

In the 7th century BCE, when the Assyrian capital in Mesopotamia was destroyed by the Medes and Babylonians, the Assyrians founded a small village in the north of Caria where Aphrodisias now stands; here, they built a wooden temple to Ishtar, the Mesopotamian goddess of love and beauty. Long considered a legend, a reflection of this story was unearthed when reliefs depicting the Assyrian king Ninus and his wife Semiramis were discovered in the Civil Basilica. These works, currently housed in the excavation team's depot, will be put on display in days to come.

The Ionic columns of the Temple of Aphrodite and the Civil Basilica have withstood centuries of wear.

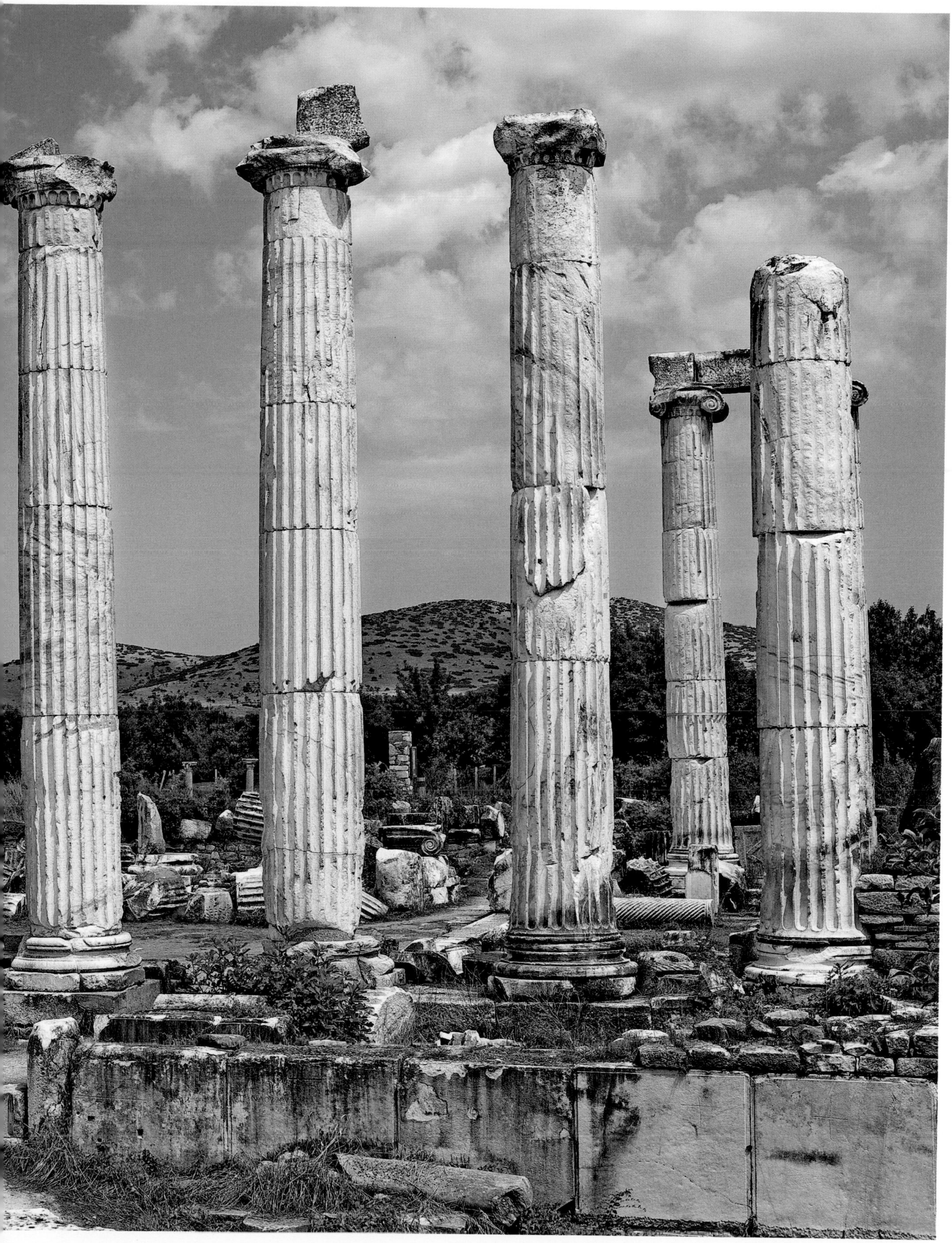

Doorframes at the courtyard entrance.

The Temple of Aphrodite and the Civil Basilica, seen from the west.

Several different styles were used in the construction of the ancient temple. One style used here is the pseudodipteral style, in which the rows of columns that entirely surround the structure are twice as distant as usual from the inner room, called the *cella,* where the statue of the god or goddess is located, thus lending the whole a more magnificent and imposing air. There were thirteen columns down the long sides of the temple and eight columns along the short sides. Only marble was used in the construction of the temple, including the roof and the roofing tile.

It was the city's true founder, Zoilos, who had the Temple of Aphrodite constructed in the 1st century BCE. In the year 130 CE, during the reign of the Roman emperor Hadrian, the garden walls, called *temenos,* and the monumental entry building on the east were added to the structure.

Columns in the Ionic style.

The cult statue of Aphrodite stood in the holy central room, called the *cella* or *naos,* which only the male priests serving at the temple could enter. The temple served as a place of pilgrimage, and it had its own special right of sanctuary in addition to the sanctuary rights of the city itself: anyone who took shelter in this sanctuary had the right to be protected against the sanctions of local authorities.

When the city of Aphrodisias accepted Christianity in the 5th century CE, this "pagan" temple underwent a number of changes. For instance, through a very arduous process, the columns along the short sides of the temple were added to those on the long sides, and the *cella* was entirely done away with. High walls were erected all around the building, thus creating a classic three-naved church pattern, and an apse and narthex were added on the eastern and western sides, respectively. Wooden columns were added on the marble ones, forming a roofing system made of wood and then covered over with baked clay tiles. A courtyard or atrium was built in front of the narthex, and a seating area called a *sintranon* was created for the choir by adding theater-style steps inside the apse. The walls of the vaulted section of the *sintranon* were painted with images of Jesus, Mary, Gabriel, and Michael; these paintings have been closed to the public by means of a roof and doors, so that they may be better preserved. When the church was made, the cult statue of Aphrodite was broken apart and used as a building stone in a structure on the southern side; this statue, found during the course of the excavations, is on display in the Aphrodisias Museum.

View from the east.

The church was in use until the 11th century, but was then burned down during the second Seljuk raid on the city. Having become a complete ruin following subsequent earthquakes, the church was visited in the year 1156 by Tornikos, the priest of the Church of Saint John of the Ephesus Metropolite. The words that this priest said on the occasion of his visit have gone down in history: "In the cathedral where once resounded the hymns of the choir, there now sings naught but the owl."

Cult statue of Aphrodite as the Mother Goddess.

11. THE STADIUM

Located on the city's north side and dated to the first half of the 1st century CE, the Aphrodisias stadium is antiquity's largest and best-preserved stadium. It is, in fact, among the ancient world's most important structures, as well as being the most magnificent work in the city. The stadium's two ends are semi-circular ellipses, and its seating area or *cavae* could hold 30,000 spectators. The ellipse plan allowed all of the spectators to see the events without difficulty. The stadium as a whole is 270 meters (886 feet) in length and 59 meters (194 feet) in width, while the course inside the stadium is 178 meters (584 feet) in length and 40 meters (131 feet) in width. At both ends of the structure is a tunnel used by the athletes and called *sphendonai;* the tunnel on the west side was blocked off while the city walls were being built. The tunnels each have a relief on their arch's keystone: the west tunnel's relief depicts Hermes, while the east's depicts Hercules. The rows of seats are divided up by 40 sets of stairs, or *kerkides*. The seating area as a whole is 12 meters (39 feet) in height and ornamented with lion's paws. There were two small lodges in the center of the longer sections of the *cavae,* and these would be used by the city's priests and bureaucrats, by those who had arranged the games, and by those who had provided financial support and who made animal sacrifices. On top of the seats are inscribed the names of the city's notables, guests from neighboring cities, and certain occupational organizations; this

The Aphrodisias Stadium, the city's most magnificent structure, seen from the west.

*The stadium's interior course, where
competitions were held, seen from the west.*

*Northwestern view of the stadium
and the marble seats.*

View of the stadium from the west.

amounted to a sort of combined ticket. The back seats were reserved for women.

Stadiums were generally used for track-and-field events, though when necessary they would also be used for other sorts of competitions as well as for public voting purposes. The most magnificent games held at the stadium were known as the Aphrodeisia Isolympia. An inscription unearthed during excavations in Aphrodisias mentions how, in the year 180 CE, money for the games was donated from the treasury of the Temple of Aphrodite. Until the 2nd century CE, the gladiatorial and wild beast combats which took place as part of the games held for the cult of the Roman emperors necessitated the erection of temporary barriers before the seating area. Before the games would begin, there would be ceremonial processions followed by animal sacrifices. A number of reliefs depicting gladiators have been discovered from this period. Following an earthquake that

caused serious damage to the theater in the 7th century CE, the stadium's semi-circular eastern part was made fully circular by the addition of walls and used as an arena. The rows of seats, once also used as shops and depots, were constructed on inclined vaults. In later periods, these spaces were used as private residences.

The city walls of Aphrodisias were constructed rather hastily in the 360s CE. Owing to this fact, the stones of the walls are made up of remnants of unused structures, particularly those destroyed by earthquakes, which were taken without regard to what they had originally been. Among the ruins of the city walls, archaeologists have found a number of fragmentary statues and inscriptions. The stadium was included within the city walls as a last-minute decision. A good example of the hodgepodge makeup of the city walls is the friezes that can be seen on the walls to the north of the stadium.

The city walls standing against the stadium.

12. THE MONUMENTAL GATE (TETRAPYLON)

When we look at the city plan of Aphrodisias, we see that there are two main roads. The north-south road is the one that runs from the northern gate down to the theater. On the west side of this road, in the eastern section of the Temple of Aphrodite, lies a magnificent building. It is called the Tetrapylon, meaning "four gates", as it is made up of four groups of four columns each, and in fact served as a ceremonial gateway. A wooden gate opening from east to west once lay between the structure's arched eastern pediment with reliefs of Nike, Eros, and animal figures among its carved acanthus leaves and the broken triangle of its western pediment. Immediately after the gate, high walls on both sides extended approximately 70 meters (230 feet) to north and south before turning westwards to form a large courtyard extending up to the Temple of Aphrodite. Ceremonial processions would enter from the road and gather in the courtyard in back, from which point they would proceed to enter the temple. The Tetrapylon, in whose construction several different techniques and styles were used, also saw use as a site for splendid parades and shows for visitors to the city of Aphrodisias.

View from the South.

The western pediment.

The western pediment.

Hunting scene on the western pediment.

View from the east.

The Tetrapylon, 80% of whose unique architecture and statuary has been unearthed, was restored by Austrian and Turkish experts between 1985 and 1990, when Professor Kenan T. Erim was the leader of the excavation work; this counts as among Turkey's most important restoration projects. Completed on 18 October 1990, the restoration's opening ceremony was attended by Turkish president Turgut Özal. Prof. Erim passed away shortly after the ceremony, on 3 November 1990. The humble grave just to the south of the ceremonial gate is Prof. Erim's final resting place. In his own words, he lies "in the arms of his love".

The western and eastern pediments.

13. THE SEBASTEION

In classical antiquity, religious belief was founded upon a polytheistic system of gods and goddesses. This belief system, sometimes referred to as "paganism", found one of its material expressions in temples dedicated to various gods and goddesses. In the time of the Roman Empire, living emperors were also exalted to the level of deities, with temples being dedicated to them as well. These temples dedicated to the imperial cult were known as sebasteion, a word derived from the Greek σεβαστός (*sebastos*), meaning "venerable one". This word was also used as a title by a number of emperors.

The Sebasteion of Aphrodisias is a work without parallel in the ancient world. The structure is in fact a sort of complex, consisting of an entry building opening onto the north-south road, a holy path with three-storey porticoes on both sides, and a Temple of Augustus at the end of this path. According to an inscription on the structure, it was dedicated to Aphrodite and to the *gens Julia* or first Roman emperors Augustus, Tiberius, Claudius, and Nero. Excavations on the Sebasteion began in 1979, and the structure was completely uncovered in 1983. The fifteen houses that stood here prior to the excavation were nationalized and relocated to the village of Yeni Geyre. A portion of the Sebasteion's south portico has been restored, giving visitors a general idea of the original appearance of the structure.

Construction of the complex began in the time of the Emperor Tiberius (r. 14–37 CE), with certain main structures damaged in earthquakes during construction being completed under Claudius (r. 41–54 CE) and the entire structure seeing completion in the time of Nero (r. 54–68 CE).

According to Roman state policy, captured land would be granted to Roman patricians, who would work the land and pay a portion of their earnings as tax to Rome. Zoilos, the second founder of the city of Aphrodisias, was not a patrician; owing to his personal past, however, he was a man with certain privileges. After Zoilos' death, the Sebasteion's expenses were met by two Roman patrician families. The north portico was dedicated by the brothers Menander and Eusebes, together with Eusebes' wife Apphias, while the south portico and the Temple of Augustus were dedicated by the brothers Diogenos and Attalus. This was effectively a way of emphasizing these Roman patrician families' presence in the city of Aphrodisias.

Built entirely of marble, the Sebasteion complex is lined on both sides by three-storey porticoes, whose floors are also laid with marble. The three storeys were built, in order, using the Doric, Ionic, and Corinthian styles. The first floor is made up of rooms containing a door and window, while the rich reliefs between the columns of the second and third storeys lent a certain grandeur and importance to the structure. The reliefs on the second storey depicted various mythological subjects, while those on the third storey represented the Roman imperial family and the various ethnicities under Roman rule.

The buildings were destroyed in the earthquake that occurred in the 7th century CE, and after undergoing repairs were subsequently used for handicraft workshops, such as glassblowing, and as a marketplace.

Around 200 reliefs were used in the decoration of the Sebasteion; only 80 of these, however, have been uncovered during the excavations, either in whole or in part. All of these works are on display in the Sevgi Gönül Sebasteion wing of the Aphrodisias Museum, designed by the architect Cengiz Bektaş and supported by the Geyre Foundation.

View of the eastern corner of the southern portico after restoration.

Nero and his mother Agrippina the Younger.
Agrippina is crowning her young son Nero with a laurel wreath and carrying a cornucopia, symbolic of good fortune and abundance. Nero wears the distinctive armor of Roman commanders, and there is a helmet lying on the ground at his feet. This relief represents the accession to the throne of Nero in the year 54 CE, and has been dated to before the year 59 CE, when Nero had Agrippina killed.

General view from the east.

The North Portico.

The North Portico after restoration.

The Three Graces, depicted in a typical Hellenistic style. The Three Graces were the servants of Aphrodite, and are depicted on the goddess' cult statue in Aphrodisias in the same poses as seen here. Their names reveal their characters: Euphrosyne ("joy"), Aglaea ("splendor"), and Thalia ("verdancy").

Aeneas' Flight from Troy. Aphrodite's son Aeneas was one of the few to escape the destruction of Troy. With the help of his mother, he rescued his son Julus Ascanius, his wife, and his father Anchises, whom he carried out of the burning city on his shoulders. After a long series of adventures, Aeneas founded the city of Rome. It is for this reason that the Roman emperors considered Aeneas and his mother Aphrodite as their ancestors.

The Cretan ethnicity.

Claudius and Britannia. In this relief depicting the power of the Roman Empire, Claudius is conquering Britain, depicted as a female slave.

Claudius with his wife Agrippina the Younger and the people.

KΛAYΔIOΣ
ΔPOYΣOΣ KAIΣAΡ
ΣEBAΣTOΣ

HΛIOΣ

Claudius, Lord of the Land and the Sea. Depicted here as a god, Claudius is displaying himself to mortals, stepping forward as his mantle flows in waves around him. The emperor is taking a ship's rudder from the mermaid-like female triton rising up from below, while from the other figure he is taking a cornucopia filled with the fruits of earth. The idea that this scene reflects is the god-emperor's assurance of prosperity on land and sea. Overall, the relief is a laudatory visual expression of the emperor's function as a universal savior and divine protector.

14. THE APHRODISIAS MUSEUM

During the initial excavations carried out by Professor Kenan T. Erim, the very numerous works that were unearthed had to be stored in relatively primitive depots. Hoping to answer the felt need for an Aphrodisias Museum, the Turkish Ministry of Culture and Tourism began a museum-building project under the architect Erten Altaban.

Expenses for the museum's construction and exhibition spaces were procured chiefly from the Ministry of Culture and Tourism, as well as from the National Geographic Society, other donors, and from Prof. Erim himself, while the restoration of the works and preparation for their display was handled by the excavation team in 1976, with grants from the National Endowment for the Humanities in Washington, DC.

Restorations were completed with assistance from Muhittin Uysal and Reha Arıcan of the Istanbul Archaeology Museum's restoration department, after which the statues were relocated to the museum. The design of the museum grounds was completed with the participation of Altan Türe, the museum's first curator, and the journalist Özgen Acar. The Aphrodisias Museum was opened to the public in June of 1979.

In the year 2008, the Aphrodisias Excavations Geyre Foundation, based in Istanbul, added the Sebasteion-Sevgi Gönül Hall to the museum. The same foundation had the museum renovated in the year 2009.

Numerous statues and reliefs unearthed during the course of excavations are on display in the museum, which should be navigated by first turning to the right after entering.

The tondo busts seen on the wall on the left of the entryway are highly original works. Dated to the 5th century CE, they were found in the house next to the Sebasteion. In antiquity, the busts of certain state officials and artists would be shown within a circular medallion bearing reliefs; these were known as *tondo*s. The names underneath reveal the depicted person's identity. The busts in the museum's entrance are depictions of the famed mathematician Pythagoras, the Athenian statesman and general Alcibiades, Alexander the Great, the poet Pindar, and a local philosopher. The fact that there is no name inscribed underneath the bust of the latter raises the possibility that it is a depiction of the owner of the house in which these busts were found. On the wall opposite the busts are displayed items belonging to prehistoric Aphrodisias.

THE HALL OF EMPERORS

Statue of the Emperor Domitian: Following the death of the Emperor Domitian (r. 81–96 CE), statues of him were forbidden in line with the Roman Senate's passage of *damnatio memoriae* against him, and as a result, this statue was discovered broken into pieces in the orchestra section of the theater. We learn from the inscription on the base of the statue that it is the work of Diogenes the son of Eukelos.

Across from the statue of Domitian is a headless statue of an emperor clad in armor and signed "Alexander Aster". Also in this hall are a number of portait heads made between the 1st century BCE and the 5th century CE.

The statue of a standing, toga-clad young man on the opposite wall represents a patrician state official and is known as "Young Togatus". The statue's riding boots show that it is a representation of an equestrian soldier. The statue of a standing young girl beside Young Togatus has sometimes been called "Madonna" due to her melancholy gaze. This statue is an example of the type called *puducitia*, meaning "chaste". Next to it stands a statue of a priest.

Statue of a young man in a toga.
This piece was discovered in 1983, shattered into thirty pieces by the columned façade of the Agora Gate which blocks off the eastern side of the South Agora (Portico of Tiberius).

THE ZOILOS CORRIDOR

The works in this section consist of reliefs found on the memorial tomb of Zoilos, whose story is recounted towards the beginning of this book, and, belonging to the so-called "Second Classical Period" of the early Roman Empire, have been dated to approximately 30 CE. The remaining architectural elements of the memorial tomb have yet to be discovered; nevertheless, an idea concerning the structure as a whole can be arrived at through comparative techniques. Based on this, the memorial tomb must have been a temple-like structure atop a high podium. The reliefs on display surrounded the entirety of this podium, and there were also inscriptions relating Zoilos' life and the honorary titles he was granted by the city. The events depicted in the reliefs proceed in order, beginning with Zoilos' arrival in

Aphrodisias from Rome. The titles granted to Zoilos—among which were such as *Andreas* ("bravery") and *Time* ("honor")—were engraved above the figures in the reliefs. In the corners are seated figures, among them the goddess Roma and Aion, a deity representing eternity.

Aion, a deity representing eternity.

The goddess Roma.

THE MELPOMENE HALL

In this hall are exhibited the monumental statues of Apollo and Melpomene, the muse of tragedy, which were found in the theater, as well as statues of various state officials.

The realistic statues of boxers on display in the passage from the Melpomene Hall to the Odeon Hall were also discovered in the course of excavations on the theater.

THE ODEON HALL

The seated statues in this hall represent philosophers and poets and are among the many unique works of Aphrodisias' Sculptors' Academy. On the right side just as one enters the hall is a statue meant to represent the people, as we understand from the inscription on the statue's base: "Dedicated to the people by the people's council". The statue in the corner, depicted as sitting atop a large rock, is a representation of the god Apollo. Directly across from this figure of Apollo are busts representing various philosophers and scientists of antiquity.

There is, for instance, a statue of a seated male representing a philosopher who cannot be positively identified due to the statue's lack of a head; this statue was found in the Bouleuterion's stage building.

THE HALL OF UNFINISHED WORKS

Moving a bit forwards towards the corner, we see a number of varied pieces of sculpture. This collection includes works without parallel in the world's museums: the unfinished works of Aphrodisias' Sculptors' Academy.

Immediately on the left is a statue of a standing clerk holding a bottle of ink; the head was never finished, and as a result, it is very large in comparison with the body. Ahead of this work is an unfinished relief depicting an athlete, beside which is a relief of Dionysus and opposite which is a relief of Artemis. Hermes is

also here: a young man's head atop a large rock. Another part of this collection is the statue of a drunken satyr lying down. The various statues' unfinished state is perhaps a result of either disagreements over fees or of the death of the artist.

Along the length of the corridor we can also see a statue of a seated Aphrodite, half of which has disappeared; a relief depicting a soldier wearing eastern garb; and the gravestone of a person whose job was to inspect prices in the marketplace for the city municipality. Turning right at the end of the corridor, we see a helmeted head of Athena decorated with rams' heads as well as displays of coins from different periods.

Following the statues on display along the length of the corridor, which turns toward the left, we come to the wing known as the Sebasteion-Sevgi Gönül Hall.

THE SEBASTEION "SEVGİ GÖNÜL" HALL

The reliefs on display here are fascinating works that were once located between the columns of the second and third storeys of the Sebasteion.

THE ACHILLES AND PENTHESILEA HALL

While moving from the Sevgi Gönül Hall to the Hall of Aphrodite, there is a statue on the right side showing a satyr playing with the child Dionysus. In the center of this room is another statue, one representing Achilles and Penthesilea. This is a depiction of a legend from the Trojan War, during the course of whose head-to-head fights occurred one between the Greek hero and the Amazonian queen Penthesilea. Achilles was unaware of Penthesilea's identity owing to the helmet she wore, and it was only after she fell to his sword that he removed her helmet and realized that she was, in fact, a beautiful woman. This group of statues, which is a highly important work of ancient sculpture, depicts Achilles holding Penthesilea as she falls down dying. The sword wound underneath Penthesilea's right breast was originally painted so as to represent blood.

A satyr playing with the child Dionysus.

A statue head depicting Aphrodite as the goddess of love and beauty.

THE HALL OF APHRODITE

The statues of Achilles and Penthesilea and the satyr and Dionysus are in the central hall, which is the penultimate room, located just before the hall that we encounter as we leave the Sebasteion Hall.

In the middle of this hall is a statue of Aphrodite in her incarnation as a mother goddess. The statue's head was destroyed by early Christians, but we can get an idea of its appearance from the bust of Aphrodite located directly opposite, which was discovered in the theater. On the front of the statue of the goddess are reliefs depicting, at the very top, Zeus and Hera; below them, Helios (the Sun) and Selene (the Moon); and, at the bottom, the birth of Aphrodite. The figures of Eros at the very bottom seem to

depict Hades, as we can understand from the torches held upside down in their hands.

The other statues in the hall are works depicting priests and various representations of the people.

The reliefs on both sides of the exit hall are from a late period and were used as ornamentations on the capitals of pilasters; these are very important examples of late-period sculpture. On the right side at the end of the corridor is a seasonal relief in which Eros is depicted alongside the different seasons.

The priestess Claudius Antonia Tatianna.